Susie,

So glad we're neighbors! I will always remember when you brought the peach tea to me after my miscarriage. Thank you — it meant so much!

Sara

Hebrews 12:2

Nuggets

Establishing a Daily Quiet Time

SARA HIXON

WestBow Press
A DIVISION OF THOMAS NELSON

Copyright © 2013 Sara Hixon.

All rights reserved. No part of this book may be used or reproduced by any means, graphic, electronic, or mechanical, including photocopying, recording, taping or by any information storage retrieval system without the written permission of the publisher except in the case of brief quotations embodied in critical articles and reviews.

WestBow Press books may be ordered through booksellers or by contacting:

WestBow Press
A Division of Thomas Nelson
1663 Liberty Drive
Bloomington, IN 47403
www.westbowpress.com
1-(866) 928-1240

Because of the dynamic nature of the Internet, any web addresses or links contained in this book may have changed since publication and may no longer be valid. The views expressed in this work are solely those of the author and do not necessarily reflect the views of the publisher, and the publisher hereby disclaims any responsibility for them.

Any people depicted in stock imagery provided by Thinkstock are models, and such images are being used for illustrative purposes only. Certain stock imagery © Thinkstock.

All Scripture quotations, unless otherwise indicated, are taken from the Holy Bible, New International Version®. NIV®. Copyright © 1973, 1978, 1984 by International Bible Society. Used by permission of Zondervan. All rights reserved.

ISBN: 978-1-4497-8797-4 (sc)
ISBN: 978-1-4497-8798-1 (e)

Library of Congress Control Number: 2013904369

Printed in the United States of America

WestBow Press rev. date: 3/21/2013

Table of Contents

Foreword		vii
Preface		ix
Acknowledgements		x
Introduction		xii
Day 1:	Quiet Time	1
Day 2:	Peace	3
Day 3:	My Eternal Home	4
Day 4:	God's Word—Our Spiritual Food	5
Day 5:	God's Forgiveness	7
Day 6:	Hide His Word in Your Heart	9
Day 7:	Renewing Your Mind with His Word	11
Day 8:	Dealing with Anxiety	13
Day 9:	Prayer	15
Day 10:	Adoration	16
Day 11:	Thanksgiving	18
Day 12:	Supplication	20
Day 13:	Tormenting Thoughts	22
Day 14:	Salvation by Grace	24
Day 15:	Good Works	26
Day 16:	Is He Lord of Your Life?	28
Day 17:	Our Healer	30
Day 18:	Contentment	33
Day 19:	Forgiving Others	35
Day 20:	Decision-Making and Hearing God's Voice	37

Day 21:	Our Creator	40
Day 22:	Made in His Image	42
Day 23:	Conflict	43
Day 24:	Great and Mighty Things We Know Not Of	45
Day 25:	Life Is Not Fair!	47
Day 26:	All Things for the Good	49
Day 27:	Purpose	51
Day 28:	Caution—Complaining Is Hazardous!	53
Day 29:	Crucified with Christ	55
Day 30:	Heaven	57
Jesus: Is He Your Lord and Savior?		59
What Next?		61

Foreword

Have you ever wanted to know someone but found it difficult to spend time with that person?

Something always comes up. Interruptions, schedule conflicts, and emergencies, among other things, make it difficult to get to know this special person. We realize we are missing the benefit of the insight, wisdom, and encouragement this person could offer us. Yet change is hard, and so we feel stuck.

For most of us, trying to spend time with God is a lot like this. It can be hard to make the time. The difficulty of having a daily quiet time with God overwhelms our overscheduled lives and feels like an obligation which raises all kinds of questions. What do I do? Where do I start? What do I read?

I would like to introduce you to Sara Hixon. In the twenty-plus years my wife and I have known her, Sara consistently enjoys a successful daily quiet time. She has served God faithfully and consistently while helping to teach and train others in our church for over sixteen years. She lives a life that exemplifies the teachings of Jesus. And now, because of her walk with God and creation of this devotional, you, too, can develop a great daily quiet time with God.

I believe God put into Sara's heart the desire to write this devotional specifically to help you. Why? Because you are important to God. Because he longs to teach you. But more than that, because he longs to get to know you. He longs to spend time with you. You see, he loves you immensely. You are valuable to him.

So why not begin your journey to a life of close relationship with God by taking just a few minutes a day to read a devotional lesson from this book. Each lesson includes a Bible passage and guided prayer time. The result for you? Steady, daily growth in your walk with God.

He is ready; he is waiting for your daily quiet time with him.

Pastor Doug Bartsch
His Place Family Church
Spring, Texas

Preface

When I became a Christian on October 10, 1986, a friend (who later became my husband) gave me a thirty-day devotional book, which I read faithfully for thirty days. They say that if you do something for twenty-one days straight, it becomes a habit. Well, it definitely worked for me! Over the past twenty-six years of my Christian life, I have been blessed to spend time reading my Bible and spending time in prayer with the Lord on a regular basis. It is only by his grace that early in my Christian walk, I was blessed to establish a daily quiet time.

I wrote this book from a desire to see believers achieve the same victory, because I know it is a struggle for many Christians to find daily time with God. I believe that spending time every day reading God's Word and being with him in prayer is crucial to growing in our walk with God and to walking in victory. Think about it: How do you grow in a relationship with someone? You spend time with them. As you read God's Word, he is speaking to you through his Word, and you are getting to know him. As you pray, you speak to him and listen to him in your spirit, growing in your relationship with your heavenly Father. Your spirit is strengthened and you are ready to walk through the battles of life to victory.

Acknowledgements

I have so many people to thank for influencing my spiritual journey. All of you have touched my life and in some way had an effect on this book.

Larry, I am so blessed to have you as my husband. Our family has benefitted tremendously from your godly leadership. I know I am a better person, wife and mother because you are my spouse. I love you!

Mom, I have learned so much from you about overcoming adversity. You have always had a passion for living and a sensitivity to God that has helped you persevere through much hardship with a godly attitude. I love and admire you!

Lindsay, Daniel and Connor, you are gifts from God to your dad and I. It is a privilege to be your parents. One of the most rewarding opportunities in my life has been to raise the three of you and experience the joys and challenges of parenthood.

Pastor Doug and Kim, thank you for your uncompromising, practical teaching of God's Word and your faithful leadership of our church. Thank you for your words of encouragement regarding this devotional.

Kay, you are a mighty woman of God and a great mentor to me. Thank you for your godly example.

Linda, Tony, Beth and Vince, I love you all. Thank you, Tony, for planting the seeds of the gospel in us. You came to know him, and then we eventually all came into the kingdom of God. It was definitely a domino effect.

Susan O., you helped disciple me from the beginning of my Christian walk, and I appreciate your friendship so much. I really enjoy our walks and talks.

Susan S., you are a dear friend, and I thank you so much for the idea for the title of this book, ***Nuggets***.

My prayer partners in Moms in Prayer, what a wonderful group of godly women you are. The years we have shared praying together for our children are so precious to me.

My friends and family who read the devotional before it was published, I really appreciate your spending valuable time to read this book and provide feedback. Your suggestions were great and they helped to improve the book in many ways.

Thank you, heavenly Father, for your hand on my life and your guidance in writing this devotional. May you be glorified through its pages and in the lives of all who read it.

Introduction

May this devotional be a new beginning for you. It consists of thirty days' worth of devotionals, each containing a nugget of truth, a Bible reading passage, and a prayer section for each day. Try to read one day's devotional every day, for thirty days straight. If you miss a day, just continue the next day. My suggestion is that you have your quiet time in the morning so you will be spiritually fed and ready for the day. If you miss the morning, you still have the evening for your quiet time. However, the most important thing is to find the time that works best for you and to be consistent. If morning is best for you, have your quiet time each morning. If evening is better, have it then.

I also recommend that you read each day's devotional Scriptures in your own Bible—even though most of them appear in full in this book—so that you get used to opening your Bible and reading from God's Word daily. This practice will also help you learn the relative locations of different passages and books in the Bible. Because the passages are short, take time to think deeply and reflect on each one.

Please know that the "Prayer time" sections are guidelines for prayer during your quiet time; you need not limit your prayer time to only what is suggested. Often, when people are just learning to pray, they don't know where to begin. These sections are suggestions to get you jump-started into your prayer time with God.

After you have completed the thirty devotionals, the three Bible reading plans in the Appendices will help you continue your daily quiet times. Appendix B is a plan for reading the gospel of John in thirty more days. Appendix C is a three-month plan for reading the New Testament. Appendix D is a plan to guide you in reading the Bible chronologically over two years.

It is my prayer that, after you have finished this book, a daily quiet time with God will not only be a habit, but also a time you look forward to every day, spending time with God—the Father, the Son, and the Holy Spirit.

Dedication

This book is dedicated to all those who have struggled with having a daily time with God. May this book lead you to victory!

In memory of my dear Aunt Fran who went to be with the Lord during the editing of this book: she shined brightly for the Lord and her life was characterized by the fruit of the Spirit. Aunt Fran always had an encouraging word, including one of her last words, "Celebrate".

Day 1   4/11/16

Quiet Time

Jesus knew the importance of quiet time with his Father. In Mark 1:35, he got up early in the morning and went to a solitary place to pray. He knew he needed to be spiritually strengthened by time alone with his Father.

You may be thinking, *Why do I need to have a quiet time? I pray to God throughout the day.* In fact, you should do both of these things! My daughter, Lindsay, is a prayer warrior. No matter where we are or what we are doing, she does not hesitate to pray about anything. Just as the Bible instructs in 1 Thessalonians 5:17, she prays without ceasing. However, Lindsay also spends time alone with God each day.

The purpose of a daily quiet time is not to limit your prayers to only that specific period. It is a chance for you to get away from the distractions of life and have some concentrated time alone with your heavenly Father, much like time you spend with your spouse or close friend. You communicate with your spouse and friends on an ongoing basis. But to grow your relationship, you must also make time for just the two of you, free from distraction.

A daily quiet time will refresh you and strengthen you as you read the Word and pray to God. Some days, it will feel like a sacrifice, because your flesh wants to do other things.

But as you put God first and devote that time to him, your prayers throughout the day will be even more meaningful because you are growing closer to him. Prayer will become part of your lifestyle as you talk to him without ceasing. You will automatically go to him with your concerns, thank him, and praise him throughout each day. What an awesome opportunity to be in constant communication with the King of Kings and Lord of Lords!

Bible reading

"Very early in the morning, while it was still dark, Jesus got up, left the house and went off to a solitary place, where he prayed" (Mark 1:35).

"The times of refreshing shall come from the presence of the Lord" (Acts 3:19 KJV).

Prayer time

Praise God that he is always available to spend time with you. Ask him to help you faithfully spend time with him every day by reading his Word and praying to him. Confess your sins to him and ask his forgiveness. Thank him for his Word and how it gives you clear direction in every area of your life. Pray for your needs and the needs of others.

Day 2

Peace

When I first came to know the Lord, the first fruit of the Spirit that I experienced was great peace. A void in my life was filled. For years, I had attempted to fill this emptiness with things of this world. I had even written in my journal before entering my junior year of college: "Something is missing in my life. I'm just trying to figure out what it is." Then, I found what I had been searching for so long: Jesus, the Prince of Peace, the giver of eternal life.

Bible reading

"Come to Me all you who are weary and heavy laden and I will give you rest. Take my yoke upon you and learn from Me for I am gentle and humble in heart and you will find rest for your souls. For my yoke is easy and my burden is light" (Matthew 11:28–30).

Prayer time

Praise God that he is the Prince of Peace. Confess your sins to him and ask his forgiveness. Thank him for loving you and giving his life for you. Ask him to give you his peace and to carry your burdens. Pray for your needs and the needs of others, especially anyone you know who needs the peace of God.

Day 3

My Eternal Home

One day a minister who helped mentor me in college gave me a Scripture to memorize. Although it was long, it was the first Scripture I memorized after being saved. I often meditate on it, even now. It really puts in perspective our life here on earth.

Bible reading

"Therefore, we do not lose heart. Though outwardly we are wasting away, yet inwardly we are being renewed day by day. For our light and momentary troubles are achieving for us an eternal glory that far outweighs them all. So we fix our eyes not on what is seen, but on what is unseen. For what is seen is temporary, but what is unseen is eternal" (2 Corinthians 4:16–18).

Prayer time

Praise God that he has given you eternal life through his Son, Jesus. Confess your sins to him and ask his forgiveness. Thank him that he is renewing you, day by day, through those momentary troubles you experience. Thank him that this world is temporary, and that he has an eternal home waiting for you in heaven. Pray for your needs and for anyone you know who is going through a challenging time in their life.

Day 4

God's Word—
Our Spiritual Food

How do you feel when you skip a meal? What if you didn't eat for an entire day? You would be weak, tired, hungry, and irritable! Our spirits need food, just like our bodies. The food for our spirits is God's Word. If we miss eating our spiritual food for a day, what do you think will happen? Our spirits will be weak, tired, and hungry. That's why you need to read God's Word daily. The other day, my sixteen-year-old son, Daniel, was kind of grumpy. Because it was summer, our routines were a little more relaxed, so I asked, "Have you had your quiet time today?" He thought for a minute and then replied, "No, I haven't. Why do you ask? Am I irritable?" I responded, "Yes, a little." He immediately sat down, read his Bible, and prayed. The rest of the day was much better for all of us.

Bible reading

"Jesus answered, 'It is written: "Man does not live on bread alone, but on every word that comes from the mouth of God"'" (Matthew 4:4).

Prayer time

Praise God for his Word that gives us spiritual nourishment each day. Confess your sins and ask forgiveness. Thank him that we live in a country where we have the freedom to have Bibles and read his Word without secrecy. Pray for your needs and the needs of others.

Day 5   4/15

God's Forgiveness

Part of our prayer time each day is for confessing our sins and asking his forgiveness for them. When you were saved, you asked God to forgive you of your sins. You put your trust in Jesus because his blood paid the price for all of your sins, past, present, and future. After we come to salvation, when we sin, our fellowship with God—not our relationship—is hindered. We are still his children; however, our sin stands in the way of our fellowship with him. Think of a parent and child. When a child disobeys his father, there is a disruption in their fellowship, but the child is still the father's son. The son should confess his sin to his father, just as we should confess our sins to our heavenly Father. Then our heavenly Father will forgive, just as our earthly fathers should, and fellowship will be restored.

Bible reading

"If we confess our sins, he is faithful and just and will forgive us our sins and purify us from all unrighteousness" (1 John 1:9).

Prayer time

Praise God that Jesus, your Savior, saved you from a life of sin and darkness. Confess your sins and ask his forgiveness. Thank Jesus for dying on the cross and paying for your sins with his blood. Pray for your needs and the needs of others.

Day 6

Hide His Word in Your Heart

How do we hide his Word in our hearts? We start by memorizing Scripture to get his Word into our minds. Then, after much meditation, his Word enters our hearts as we apply it to our daily lives. While I was in physical therapy school, my friend Susan and I memorized Scripture together. We would write down a verse on an index card and carry it around with us all week. As we waited for classes to start, we would pull out our cards and read the verse, trying to memorize a little bit more each day. By the end of the week, we would have a new verse hidden in our hearts. I am so thankful for that time of concentrated Scripture memorization. Throughout my Christian life, having his Word readily available for myself and others in times of need has really helped.

My husband, Larry, is constantly memorizing and meditating on Scripture. He always has a verse written down on a small piece of paper in his pocket. He takes it out several times a day to read it over. You might want to begin memorizing some of the verses in this devotional. Pick the ones that really speak to your heart, and start learning one each week. It will change your life.

Bible reading

"I have hidden your word in my heart that I might not sin against you" (Psalm 119:11).

Prayer time

Praise God for his omniscience; he is all-knowing. Confess your sins and ask forgiveness. Thank him for imparting his wisdom and knowledge to us through his Word. Thank him for any answers to prayer. Ask him to help you memorize his Word. Pray for the needs of others.

Day 7

Renewing Your Mind with His Word

Did you know that your life could be transformed by renewing your mind with God's Word? Your mind is the part of your soul that thinks. Everything we say and do first begins with a thought. The only way to change, then, is to first change what you think.

Bible reading

"Do not conform any longer to the pattern of this world, but be transformed by the renewing of your mind. Then you will be able to test and approve what God's will is—his good, pleasing and perfect will" (Romans 12:2).

Here we are told that we can be transformed by renewing our minds. How do we renew our minds? By reading Scripture, memorizing it, and meditating on it by thinking deeply and reflecting. If you struggle with anxiety, memorize verses that give direction for handling anxiety. If you struggle with anger, meditate on verses that tell you how to handle anger. If you are not sure what to do in a particular situation, study verses about wisdom and ask God for the wisdom and discipline to know and do his will. Once it renews your mind, God's Word will spill over into your emotions, your will, and your body. Then you can follow through by acting upon it. Tomorrow's topic will give you an example of how to do this.

Prayer time

Praise God for giving you his Word to bring change to your life. Confess your sins and ask forgiveness. Thank him for being faithful to you by always being there when you need him. Pray that you and another person will be transformed by renewing your mind with God's Word.

4/18

Day 8

Dealing with Anxiety

This is a biggie for me. Anxiety used to be a constant part of my life. Throughout my Christian walk, God has delivered me from much fear and worry. The biggest lesson I learned was to replace worry with prayer.

Bible reading

"Do not be anxious about anything, but in everything, by prayer and petition, with thanksgiving, present your requests to God. And the peace of God, which transcends all understanding, will guard your hearts and your minds in Christ Jesus" (Philippians 4:6–7).

Do you see the promise God offers in these verses? If we pray to him and present him with our concerns and requests, he promises to give us his peace. Learn to recognize worry as soon as it creeps into your mind. Then, repeat Philippians 4:6–7, meditating on his promise. Do as the scripture instructs: "by prayer and petition" pray, asking God to take care of your specific situation. If the worry returns, remind yourself that you have already prayed; now you just need to trust God to take care of it. If you continue to worry, repeat the steps.

I have really been put to the test about anxiety lately. Work has been quite stressful and I have found myself dealing with more worry than I have had in years. Therefore I have been lifting up my specific concerns to the Lord. When I truly trust him with each concern, it is amazing how much his peace guards my heart.

Prayer time

Praise God that he is Jehovah Shalom, which means "God is peace" (Jehovah is one of the names of God and Shalom is the Hebrew word for peace). Confess your sins and ask forgiveness. Thank him that he is able to take care of any situation you face and that he can deliver you from worry and anxiety. Pray for your needs and the needs of others.

Day 9

Prayer

You might be wondering why I have included certain elements in the prayer time sections. Jesus taught his disciples how to pray in chapter 5 of Matthew, with the Lord's Prayer. I have used the popular "ACTS" method of forming prayers that uses components of the Lord's prayer: Adoration, Confession, Thanksgiving and Supplication. We will study each of these types of prayer on upcoming days.

Bible reading

"This, then, is how you should pray:
'Our Father in heaven, hallowed be your name,
your kingdom come, your will be done on earth as it is in heaven.
Give us today our daily bread.
Forgive us our debts, as we also have forgiven our debtors.
And lead us not into temptation, but deliver us from the evil one'" (Matthew 6:9–13).

Prayer time

Now say the Lord's Prayer and think about each phrase as you pray it to your heavenly Father.

Day 10

Adoration

Let's start with the *A* in ACTS: adoration. In the Lord's Prayer, Jesus teaches us to begin our prayer by acknowledging our heavenly Father and proclaiming his holiness. If you have been following the suggestions for your prayer time each day, you have already been praising God and showing adoration for Him. Praise begins with just thinking of an attribute of God or a word that describes who he is, such as: loving, omniscient (all-knowing), omnipotent (all-powerful), wise, merciful, or provider, deliverer, protector, creator. Then, praise him for who he is. How do we do that? Think about someone in your life you could praise, such as a daughter who is helpful around the house. What would you say? How about, "Daughter, you are so helpful. I appreciate that you help out when you see a need." You acknowledge who she is and praise her for her helpfulness.

If you ever struggle with how to praise the Lord, go to the book of Psalms and choose a psalm to pray out loud to God. David really knew how to praise the Lord and to show his adoration for his heavenly Father. Here is a passage to begin today's prayer time with adoration. You can make it even more direct by replacing the references to God with "you."

Bible reading

"Praise the Lord. How good it is to sing praises to our God, how pleasant and fitting to praise him! The Lord builds up Jerusalem; he gathers the exiles of Israel. He heals the brokenhearted and binds up their wounds. He determines the number of the stars and calls them each by name. Great is our Lord and mighty in power; his understanding has no limit" (Psalms 147–5).

Prayer time

You have just praised God by praying the above Scripture. Confess your sins and thank him for what he is doing in your life. Ask God to help you praise him more, and pray for the needs of others.

Day 11

Thanksgiving

We already learned about confession, the C of ACTS, back on Day 5, so now we will move on to T, thanksgiving. How do you feel when someone you help time and time again seldom or never thanks you? And how do you feel when helping someone who always thanks you? It makes you want to keep helping them, doesn't it?

In our Bible reading today, Jesus shows us how much he appreciates and notices when someone says "thank you".

Bible reading

"As he was going into a village, ten men who had leprosy met him. They stood at a distance and called out in a loud voice, 'Jesus, Master, have pity on us!' When he saw them, he said, 'Go, show yourselves to the priests.' And as they went, they were cleansed. One of them, when he saw he was healed, came back, praising God in a loud voice. He threw himself at Jesus' feet and thanked him—and he was a Samaritan. Jesus asked, 'Were not all ten cleansed? Where are the other nine? Was no one found to return and give praise to God except this foreigner?' Then he said to him, 'Rise and go; your faith has made you well'" (Luke 17:12–19).

Always take time to thank God for all he has done for you,

just as we've done in each day's prayer time. Thank him for his provision in your life: health, food, clothing, friendship, finance, family, etc. Remember that all we have is his, anyway. We are just stewards of what he has given us here on earth. Thank him for all the prayers he has answered. Cultivate a thankful heart. It will lead you down the path of fulfillment and contentment.

Prayer time

Praise God that he is our healer. Confess your sins. Thank him for his provision. Ask him to help you have a more thankful heart. Pray for the needs of others.

4/22

Day 12

Supplication

Today we conclude our study of the ACTS method by looking at the S, supplication. To supplicate is to humbly ask, especially by prayer. Jesus tells us to use the Lord's Prayer to ask for our daily bread and for God not to lead us to temptation, but deliver us from evil. These are supplications.

One way you can keep track of prayer requests and answers is by starting a prayer journal. I started one over twenty years ago, and it has been a blessing to be able to look back and see all of God's answers to my prayers. A journal is a great aid to being diligent in your prayer life and praying with persistence. I like to organize my prayers by days of the week. That way, I know I'm praying over each request at least once per week. For each day of the week, I record prayer requests on one page; on the opposite page, I leave space for answers to those prayers. Appendix A is a sample journal layout to get you started, should you choose to keep your own prayer journal.

Bible reading

"This is the confidence we have in approaching God: that if we ask anything according to his will, he hears us. And if we know that he hears us—whatever we ask—we know that we have what we asked of him" (1 John 5:14–15).

Prayer time

Praise God for being your provider. Confess your sins. Thank him for providing your daily bread and your other needs. Humbly ask him to provide for any specific needs you have, and for the needs of others.

4/23

Day 13

Tormenting Thoughts

There was a time in my life, while my children were still young, that I feared they or my husband might die an early death. It was absolute torment from the enemy. These thoughts would often come out of nowhere and fear would grip me. I always took time to pray, but the thoughts would eventually return.

Total deliverance came one day when I was reading Romans 8.
I read the following verses and God spoke his truth loud and clear.

Bible reading

"No, in all these things we are more than conquerors through him who loved us. For I am convinced that neither death nor life, neither angels nor demons, neither the present nor the future, nor any powers, neither height nor depth, nor anything else in all creation, will be able to separate us from the love of God that is in Christ Jesus our Lord" (Romans 8:37–39).

With these verses, God showed me that nothing could ever separate me from his love. His love will carry me through whatever challenges I face in the future. He will never leave me or forsake me; nothing that happens in this life can change that. I realized that if anything did happen to my family, God would be right there with me, surrounding me with his love, comfort, and guidance. My loneliness and loss would be eased by his great love for me. God's Word totally transformed my life in this area.

Prayer time

Praise God that he is all-powerful. Nothing can separate you from his love. Rejoice that he will carry you through anything. Confess your sins and ask forgiveness. Thank him for giving you peace and delivering you from fear of things to come. Pray for your needs and the needs of others.

4/24   *Day 14*

Salvation by Grace

I still remember the day I first began to grasp the meaning of God's grace. Growing up, I thought salvation came through good works. Shortly after starting physical therapy school, I began attending a Bible study taught by two senior physical therapy students. One night, the subject was on salvation by grace. Our teacher asked, "Is there anything we can do in our own works to go to heaven?" In my mind I thought, "Yes, I can read my Bible, pray, help others, and go to church. These things will help me get to heaven." I looked around the room and to my amazement, everyone else was shaking their heads no. All I could think was, *Wow, I have really missed something here.* My teacher had my full attention as he read the following Scriptures.

Bible reading

"For it is by grace you have been saved, through faith—and this not from yourselves, it is the gift of God—not by works, so that no one can boast" (Ephesians 2:8–9).

You can't get much clearer than that! God makes it very clear that the only way we can be saved and go to heaven is by accepting the gift of God: salvation through Jesus Christ. Jesus paid for our salvation with his own innocent blood. The Bible says that "all our righteous acts are like filthy rags"

(Isaiah 64:6). How could we be so mixed up as to think that anything we did could be good enough to get us into heaven? The Bible is clear. It is by his grace alone.

Prayer time

Praise God that he is a generous and loving Father who gives us more love than we deserve. Confess your sins and thank him for being so faithful and just as to forgive us our sins. Thank Jesus for dying in your place for your sins. Pray for your needs and for the salvation of any unsaved friends or family.

Day 15

4/25

Good Works

So where do good works come in? God tells us that "faith by itself, if it is not accompanied by action, is dead…. do you want evidence that faith without deeds is useless?… You see that [Abraham's] faith and his actions were working together, and his faith was made complete by what he did" (James 2:17, 20, 22). In these passages, God shows us that our good deeds are the evidence of our faith. Our motivation for doing good deeds is not getting into heaven, because if we have asked Jesus to be our Lord and Savior and surrendered our lives to him, we already know we are heaven-bound. Rather, our motivation for good deeds is our love for God and gratitude for how much he has given us. Our deeds are evidence of our faith and an expression of our love for God and for others.

God has deeds for you to do; you were created to complete these assignments for him. As you carry them out, you will put your faith to action. Today's Bible reading directly follows the verses we read yesterday.

Bible reading

"For we are God's workmanship, created in Christ Jesus to do good works, which God prepared in advance for us to do" (Ephesians 2:10).

Prayer time

Praise God that he is your loving Father and Creator. Confess your sins to him. Thank him for the good works he has prepared you to do. Ask him to help you carry them out with an obedient heart. Pray for anyone who is in need.

Day 16

Is He Lord of Your Life?

One day I noticed a flyer on the church bulletin board with the title, "Putting God First." It was accompanied by the Scripture below.

Bible reading

"But seek first his kingdom and his righteousness and all these things will be given to you as well" (Matthew 6:33).

This verse really resonated with me because when I was first saved, I didn't really understand what was happening to me. All I knew was that I wanted to put God first in every area of my life, something I had never done before. I knew that, somehow, he would take care of the rest. This is exactly what the Scripture promises: that when we put God first, he takes care of the rest! If we trust him with our time by doing what he wants us to do, even when we are busy, he blesses us with the time to accomplish the things that we put on hold for him. The same goes for our finances: when we give him our tithes and offerings, he makes our remaining money go even further by keeping our clothes from wearing out, our cars from breaking down, and so on. Another way to put God first is having quiet time with him; we put him first in the day, possibly sacrificing something else that needs to be done. However, because we put him first, he orders and directs the events of the day, making our time more productive.

Prayer time

Praise God for being trustworthy and keeping his promises. Confess your sins to him. Thank him for all the promises he has made you in his Word. Thank him for answered prayers. Pray for your needs and the needs of others.

1/27

Day 17

Our Healer

The pastor of a church we attended many years ago had experienced many great miracles in his family; God had healed their bodies. He taught us about the many healings Jesus performed and that we should come to God in faith for our healing. Sometimes God heals supernaturally, sometimes he uses doctors and medicine, and sometimes he combines both. Other times, he performs the ultimate healing by taking people to heaven to be free of sickness forever. We do not know his timing or methods, or whether our healing will take place on this earth. However, we do know that it pleases him for us to come to him in faith. Hebrews 11:6 says, "And without faith it is impossible to please God, because anyone who comes to him must believe that he exists and that he rewards those who earnestly seek him."

In our family, we pray for healing whenever sickness or disease attacks. I will share with you a time when God healed my son Daniel supernaturally. One of Daniel's top front baby teeth came in very crooked, resulting in a crossbite; when he bit down, the top tooth was positioned behind his bottom tooth. In fact, it angled so extremely toward the back of his mouth that people would often comment, "Oh, is he missing a tooth?" I prayed regularly for Daniel, asking God to straighten his tooth.

When he was four years old, I took him to a pediatric dentist, who recommended a type of bracing to correct the tooth and prevent jaw malalignment. The doctor tried to put a band on Daniel's back molar, but Daniel was in tears. I said, "No, I don't want to put him through this." We went home and continued to pray. One night about two months later, as I helped Daniel brush his teeth before bedtime, I noticed that his crooked tooth had actually moved to be positioned in front of his lower bottom tooth! We were so excited. As the days went on, the tooth got straighter and straighter. By the time we returned to the dentist for Daniel's next checkup, the tooth was perfectly straight. The dentist asked us what happened. I told him it was a miracle, that we had prayed and prayed and God had healed Daniel's tooth. He responded, "It sure is a miracle. In all my twenty years as a dentist, I have never seen anything like this happen." We praise God to this day for the great miracle he performed for Daniel.

Bible reading

"Praise the Lord, O my soul, and forget not all his benefits—who forgives all your sins and heals all your diseases, who redeems your life from the pit and crowns you with love and compassion" (Psalms 103:2–4).

Prayer time

Praise God as you read the above passage from Scripture. Read it aloud, if you wish. Now confess your sins and thank him for his benefits. Pray for your needs and the needs of others.

4/28

Day 18

Contentment

It is an awesome thing to be content in your life, no matter what the situation! In a world so concerned with keeping up with the Joneses, it's easy to fall into the trap of being discontented with what you have and where you are in life. But did you know that if you make just $35,000 a year, you are among the top 5% richest people in the world?[1] That really puts things in perspective, doesn't it?

Having a thankful heart and focusing on God's goodness in your life will lead you to contentment. Don't compare yourself and your family to other people. Trust God that he knows what's best for you and your loved ones.

In the Bible, the apostle Paul writes about learning to be content.

Bible reading

"For I have learned to be content whatever the circumstances. I know what it is to be in need, and I know what it is to have plenty. I have learned the secret of being content in any and every situation, whether well fed or hungry, whether living

---

[1] You can learn where your annual income rates in the world at http://www.globalrichlist.com.

in plenty or in want. I can do everything through him who gives me strength" (Philippians 4:11–13).

"But godliness with contentment is great gain. For we brought nothing into the world, and we can take nothing out of it. But if we have food and clothing, we will be content with that" (1 Timothy 6:6).

Prayer time

Praise God that he is Jehovah Jireh, which means "God will provide." Confess your sins. Thank him that you have salvation, family, friends, food, clothing, a place to live, health, etc. Pray for your needs and the needs of others.

Day 19

Forgiving Others

Is there anyone in your life whom you need to forgive? Then don't delay. Forgiveness helps us in so many ways. If we walk with unforgiveness toward someone, then God can't forgive us! Unforgiveness can also cause sickness in our bodies because we have opened the door to the enemy. God knows that bitterness in your heart hurts you and defiles many. That is one reason he is so firm in his command for us to forgive others.

The parable about the unforgiving servant is an insightful portrait of what happens when God forgives us but we don't forgive others.

Bible reading

Read Matthew 18:21–35 in your Bible.

God is the master who forgives the huge debt. The debt in the parable represents the debt of our sins which Jesus paid for with his blood. Once we accept Jesus as our Lord and Savior, we accept his payment and our debt is removed. When we refuse to forgive people who have wronged us, we are like the unmerciful servant who was himself forgiven a huge debt he could not pay, yet who refused to forgive a minor debt someone else owed to him. Think of the minor debt as the wrong someone has done against you. It may not seem minor, and yet it is when compared to the sins we have committed against God. When we remember how much God has forgiven us, we are free to forgive others. If it is still difficult to do so, ask for his help. He is faithful and he wants to help you learn to forgive others.

Prayer time

Praise God for his mercy, which is more than we deserve. Confess your sins, especially any unforgiveness you have harbored. Thank him for revealing this to you. Ask him to help you forgive this person so you can walk in the freedom he has planned for you.

4/30

Day 20

Decision-Making and Hearing God's Voice

Understanding what the spirit, soul, and body are will help you in decision-making and in hearing God's voice. Your spirit is the part of you that will live forever. If you have accepted Jesus as your Lord and Savior, the Holy Spirit lives inside your spirit; this is where your rebirth, or born-again experience, took place to make you a new person in Christ. It is also where God speaks to you spirit to spirit.

The soul is the part of you where your mind, and emotions and will reside, and it will also live forever. It is a work in progress. If you are reading God's Word daily, your mind is being transformed; this change also spills over into your emotions and your will. The mind, emotions, and will are good, but can get in the way of hearing God's voice.

The body is your flesh and where sin resides. Like the soul, it is a work in progress. If you yield your life to the Spirit of God and let your fleshly desires die, then your body is also being transformed to become more obedient to God.

When you are making decisions, at times it is difficult to discern whether you are hearing from God or from your soul or flesh. You want to know God's will and to be led by the Holy Spirit, so you must listen to the still, small voice of the Holy Spirit. His voice brings peace; if something makes you uneasy or anxious, it is not God's voice. Also, remember that whatever God speaks will align with his Word. He will not tell you to do anything contrary to his Word. God's will and his Word are stable and peaceful.

Bible reading

"But the wisdom that comes from heaven is first of all pure; then peace-loving, considerate, submissive, full of mercy and good fruit, impartial and sincere" (James 3:17).

"But when he, the Spirit of truth, comes, he will guide you into all truth. He will not speak on his own; he will speak only what he hears, and he will tell you what is yet to come" (John 16:13).

Here are some steps for godly decision-making and hearing God's voice:

1. Ask God for wisdom (James 1:5).

2. Study God's word, specifically looking at Scriptures related to your situation (2 Timothy 3:16).

3. Wait for and follow the peaceful, still, small voice of the Holy Spirit, speaking to your spirit. God's wisdom is peaceable.(1 Kings 19:11-12, James 3:17).

Prayer time

Praise God that he is so wise and possesses all wisdom. Confess your sins. Thank him for his Word and how it helps us make decisions and hear his voice. Ask him to help you listen to and obey his voice, and for his wisdom in making specific decisions.

Day 21

Our Creator

God is the creator of this wonderful universe. He spoke it into existence in only six days. The Bible tells us that the human race can know that God exists by simply looking at what he has created: planets, stars, people, animals, etc. God is so much greater than what he created. He is more glorious than the sun, more beautiful than the mountains, and more powerful than the forces he set in motion to keep our universe in order.

Bible reading

"For since the creation of the world God's invisible qualities—his eternal power and divine nature—have been clearly seen, being understood from what has been made, so that men are without excuse" (Romans 1:20).

"The heavens declare the glory of God; the skies proclaim the work of his hands. Day after day they pour forth speech; night after night they display knowledge. There is no speech or language where their voice is not heard. Their voice goes out into all the earth, their words to the ends of the world" (Psalm 19:1).

Prayer time

Praise God that he is the Almighty, the creator of the heavens and the earth! Confess your sins. Thank him for letting you be part of his creation. Pray for your needs and the needs of others.

Day 22

Made in His Image

Not only did God create this incredible universe, he also created you. He knows everything about you. He loves you with an everlasting love. In Genesis 1:26, God says, "Let us make man in our image, in our likeness." If you ever experience a low self-image, remember that you were created in the image of God—you are fearfully and wonderfully made!

Bible reading

"For you created my inmost being; you knit me together in my mother's womb. I praise you because I am fearfully and wonderfully made; your works are wonderful, I know that full well. My frame was not hidden from you when I was made in the secret place. When I was woven together in the depths of the earth, your eyes saw my unformed body. All the days ordained for me were written in your book before one of them came to be" (Psalms 139:13–16).

Prayer time

Praise God that he is your creator. Confess your sins. Thank him that you are fearfully and wonderfully made. Pray for your needs and anyone you know who may be struggling with a low self-image.

Day 23

Conflict

How should you handle conflict God's way? Do you go directly to the person with whom you have the conflict, or should you talk to their supervisor first? Or should you perhaps talk to some of your friends about it first? Let's read to find out what God says about this.

Bible reading

"If your brother sins against you, go and show him his fault, just between the two of you. If he listens to you, you have won your brother over. But if he will not listen, take one or two others along, so that every matter may be established by the testimony of two or three witnesses" (Matthew 18:15–17).

You should first go directly to the person you are in conflict with and keep it between the two of you. If he does not listen, then you should bring one or two other people along to confront him again.

This principle for godly confrontation can greatly reduce conflict. Going behind someone's back to address an issue increases tension because you have been talking to other people instead of keeping it between the two of you. The other person could find out that you talked to someone else about the situation and wonder why you didn't go to him first. God has given us clear instructions for handling conflict and confrontation. When we do it his way, our conflicts will be handled in a godly manner without complicating the situation.

Prayer time

Praise God that he is a peacemaker. Confess your sins. Thank him for revealing to us in his Word how to handle conflict and confrontation. Pray for your needs and the needs of others.

Day 24

Great and Mighty Things We Know Not Of

God is the giver of all wisdom. He can show us things that in the natural, we would have no way of knowing. One prayer I have always prayed is for God to "show us great and mighty things we know not of" in regard to raising our children. This takes much pressure off of me as a parent. I don't have to have everything figured out. God will reveal what we need to know and when we need to know it so long as we are seeking him and putting him first in our lives. On many occasions, he has revealed to us things that we would not have known otherwise.

One example concerns our daughter, Lindsay. When Lindsay was five, she had strep throat three times within four months. The third time, I took Lindsay to the doctor just as we had done before. He gave me a prescription for antibiotics, but this time I did not get it filled. A friend had told me about a remedy that was very effective for many different illnesses, and after much prayer, we decided to give it a try. My husband and I did not think Lindsay should take another round of antibiotics because obviously the medication had not knocked out that illness. I kept the prescription on hand just in case the other remedy did not work, but praise God that it did! On our follow-up visit to the doctor, the doctor reported that Lindsay had no more strep throat. Lindsay has only had strep throat once since that time thirteen years ago. Through our friend, God showed us great things that we did not know of.

Bible reading

"Call to me and I will answer you and tell you great and unsearchable things you do not know" (Jeremiah 33:3).

Prayer time

Praise God that he is omniscient and all-knowing. Confess your sins. Thank him for revealing to you great and mighty things you would not know otherwise. Pray for your needs and the needs of others.

Day 25

Life Is Not Fair!

How many times have we thought or even said these words? We have likely heard it from our kids even more often. There is so much injustice in this world, like when teachers include on a test material they haven't even taught yet, or when you or your child are falsely accused of something. Or, even worse, when an innocent life is taken from this world by child abuse, murder, or drunk driving.

We live in a world full of sin and injustice. But no one ever told us that life would be fair. In fact, Jesus warned us that in this world we would have trouble. And yet he also gave us hope that we would overcome this trouble because he had overcome the world.

It may help to remember that if life were fair, we would have had to die for our sins. But God in his infinite mercy sent Jesus to die on the cross instead. He was sinless, but he died in our place. That's an unfairness we may rejoice in.

Bible reading

"God made him who had no sin to be sin for us, so that in him we might become the righteousness of God" (2 Corinthians 5:21).

"For the wages of sin is death, but the gift of God is eternal life in Christ Jesus our Lord" (Romans 6:23).

"I have told you these things, so that in me you may have peace. In this world you will have trouble. But take heart! I have overcome the world" (John 16:33).

Prayer time

Praise God that he is merciful! Confess your sins. Thank him that this world is not our home and that we have so much to look forward to in heaven. Pray for your needs and the needs of others.

Day 26

All Things for the Good

I love Romans 8:28; when we get a revelation of this verse and trust God that the promise is true, we can have much less frustration in our lives!

Bible reading

"And we know in all things God works for the good of those who love him, who have been called according to his purpose" (Romans 8:28).

When we realize that God truly works for the good of those who love him and are called to his purpose, we know that no matter how things might look, he is working in our behalf. If you are already running late for a destination and then take a wrong turn, you might think, *Why did that have to happen* now? God promises to work *all* things for our good, so there must be some good in that situation. Perhaps if you had not taken that wrong turn, you would have had an accident. That is a sobering thought. Somehow it makes taking a wrong turn and being late not seem like such a big deal.

I like to think of this Bible verse whenever I think of what my mom has been through regarding her health. She has had so many hospital trips this past year, and so many operations over the past seven years. My siblings and I have often wondered, "Why does she have to go through all this?" But as I consider her journey, I am reminded of the many miracles the Lord has performed in my mom's health and her life. He miraculously saved her leg when two doctors told her she needed it amputated. During one of her hospital visits, the Lord impressed upon her to stop drinking alcohol. The Holy Spirit had been convicting her about this for a while because she had a drinking problem. This time, she listened and obeyed, and she was able to stop without difficulty. God also showed us that all these hospital trips have brought about many hours of visiting with our precious mother that would not have happened otherwise. God is awesome; he truly works all things for the good of those who love him.

Prayer time

Praise God that he is good all the time. Confess your sins to him. Thank him for working things for the good in your life and think of some specific instances when you struggled and then later realized how God had worked those things for the good in your life. Pray for your needs and the needs of others.

5/7 _____ *Day 27* _____

Purpose

Have you ever wondered about your purpose—why God created you? I will not attempt to explain this in depth—there are entire books written on the subject—but I will give a couple of insights. In Ephesians 2:10 (which we studied on Day 15), we learn that "we are his workmanship, created in Christ Jesus to do good works which God prepared for us to do." Part of your purpose is to serve God and others. He tells us one of the ways to do so in Matthew 28:19: "Go and make disciples of all men, baptizing them in the name of the Father, the Son and the Holy Spirit." What big assignments these are, to do the good works God has prepared for us and to make disciples! This world is full of people who still don't know Jesus. They may number among your family, friends, coworkers, or neighbors. God wants to use you to help them to come to know him and have a personal relationship with him. The way you live speaks volumes to others.

Part of our purpose also relates to what God wants to do in us while we're on the earth. He wants to prepare us for heaven. Therefore, he wants us to grow and to be molded in his image through life experiences on earth.

Bible reading

"I know the plans I have for you," says the Lord, "plans to prosper you and not to harm you; plans to give you a future and a hope" (Jeremiah 29:11).

Prayer time

Praise your heavenly Father that he has a purpose for your life and great plans for your future! Confess your sins. Thank him that he will show you the good works he has prepared for you as you seek him daily. Thank him for molding you and shaping you and preparing you for heaven. Pray for your needs and the needs of others.

Day 28

Caution—Complaining Is Hazardous!

Complaints are all around us: a spouse complains about his or her mate, coworkers complain about their jobs, churchgoers complain about their churches, students and parents complain about a teacher. It would sometimes be easy to join in, but we must avoid this and instead cultivate thankful hearts.

God gives us many passages in the Old Testament to warn us about the seriousness of complaining. In Numbers 12, Miriam and Aaron spoke against Moses, and as a result, Miriam became leprous. In Numbers 21:4-7, the Israelites spoke against God and Moses, so the Lord sent venomous snakes among them and many Israelites died. The Israelites suffered some severe consequences as a result of their complaints.

Not too long ago, my husband and I found ourselves complaining about our medical and dental expenses. Our expenses are mostly for preventative care, however, even this cost with our insurance is very expensive. The Lord was merciful to us and showed us to be thankful that we are healthy and mostly need preventative care. When we began to be thankful for our good health, we also realized how God has provided financially for our medical and dental expenses.

So instead of complaining about your situation, thank God for your blessings. Thank him for all the good things you see in people and situations. If you have a legitimate complaint about something, take it through the proper channels and do not gossip about it along the way.

Bible reading

"Do everything without complaining or arguing so that you may become blameless and pure, children of God" (Philippians 2:14).

Prayer time

Praise God that he is your provider. Confess your sins of complaint. Thank him that he is good and blesses you with good things. Pray for your needs and the needs of others. Pray especially for the people and situations you have been complaining about, that God will help you see their good qualities and understand what they may be going through.

Day 29

Crucified with Christ

Remember the situations we talked about yesterday, the ones you may have been complaining about? God is using those situations to mold you and shape you more into his image.

Bible reading

"Consider it pure joy, my brothers, whenever you face trials of many kinds, because you know that the testing of your faith develops perseverance. Perseverance must finish its work so that you may be mature and complete, not lacking anything" (James 1:2–4).

We need to put aside the old nature that complains and resists the potter's molding and shaping hands. Don't you want to be like the apostle Paul, who walked in the revelation that his old nature died and now Christ lived in him? Because Christ lived in him, he knew he could walk in victory.

"I have been crucified with Christ and I no longer live, but Christ lives in me. The life I live in the body, I live by faith in the Son of God, who loved me and gave himself for me" (Galatians 2:20).

Prayer time

Praise God that he is patient. Confess any sin of grumbling about trials. Thank God for molding and shaping you to become more like Jesus. Pray for your needs and the needs of others.

Day 30

Heaven

This earth is not our home. If Jesus is your Lord and Savior, your citizenship is in heaven. We are just passing through this world; the time we have here is short compared to eternity. We can be heavenly minded by always remembering this. Heaven and hell are realities. What a blessing to be able to live with the confidence that we are heaven-bound!

My twelve-year-old, Connor, has a heavenly mindset. When he was younger, he was afraid of robbers. I asked him, "What is the worst thing that might happen if a robber came into our house?" He said, "I would die." I replied, "Okay, and then you would go to heaven and be with Jesus forever. Would that be bad?" He said no, and his fear of robbers lessened each day afterward. I wouldn't recommend this strategy for every parent; you have to know first whether or not this idea would make your child more fearful. Connor has been raised all of his life to know that heaven is an awesome place that we are all looking forward to reaching, so I knew it would be all right to explain things this way.

One day he told me, "I hope Jesus comes back soon." Heaven is real to Connor. Is it real to you?

Bible reading

"But our citizenship is in heaven. And we eagerly await a Savior from there, the Lord Jesus Christ, who by the power that enables him to bring everything under his control, will transform our lowly bodies so that they will be like his glorious body" (Philippians 3:20).

Prayer time

Praise God that he is in control. Confess your sins to him. Thank him for preparing a place for you in heaven and thank him that you are looking forward to that day. For friends and loved ones who do not yet know the Lord, pray that they will be saved so they may spend eternity with you in heaven.

Jesus: Is He Your Lord and Savior?

Many of you reading this book will already know Jesus as your Lord and Savior. But for those of you not yet sure whether you have been saved and are going to heaven, the first step is realizing that we are all sinners in need of a Savior. Jesus Christ was the only one who could pay the price for your sins and mine. Romans 6:23 says, "The wages of sin is death, but the gift of God is eternal life in Jesus Christ our Lord." Hebrews 9:22 tells us, "Without the shedding of blood there is no forgiveness." Jesus bought us forgiveness with his blood. There is no way to reach heaven except through Jesus. As he said in John 14:6, "I am the Way and the Truth and the Life. No man comes to the Father except by Me."

Have you asked Jesus to forgive you all the wrong things you have done and to be the Lord and Savior of your life? If you ask him, he will do it. He wants to do it; he paid a huge price for your salvation. Why not ask him today? Here is a prayer you can say if you desire to be saved.

"Heavenly Father, I am a sinner and I need your forgiveness. Please forgive me all of my sins. Thank you, Jesus, for dying on the cross and shedding your blood to pay the price of my sins. I repent and turn away from my sins, and now I turn to you, Jesus. I ask you to be my Savior and my Lord. Thank you for giving me eternal life. In Jesus's name, amen."

If you prayed that prayer and meant it in your heart, then you are now a believer! Jesus has saved you. You are a new creature in Christ. Old things are past. Behold! All things are new. I encourage you to find a church that teaches the Bible so you can grow in your relationship with your Lord and Savior, Jesus Christ.

What Next?

Congratulations! You have completed this thirty-day devotional. You are off to a great start; this is only the beginning. It is my prayer that you look forward to your time with God each day, and that by now, you have formed a habit that you will continue for the rest of your life.

The appendices of this book contain helpful resources for you as you continue your daily prayer time and Bible reading. Appendix A is a sample layout for a prayer journal, which will help you keep track of prayer requests and answers to prayer. If you still need guidelines for your prayer time, you can go back to the start of this devotional and repeat the suggestions for each day. Soon you will become comfortable praying on your own. I still use ACTS to structure my prayer time.

I have provided three Bible reading plans in appendices B, C, and D for you to continue your daily Bible reading. This will equip you with enough guided Bible reading for two and a half years. Then, you can either repeat some of the plans you have already used or find new ones. Remember, you need to read God's Word every day to stay strong, spiritually fed, and able to grow in your relationship with the Lord.

May God bless you in your journey through this life. Enjoy your quiet time with God each day. Enjoy your relationship with Him. May it grow and flourish as you spend time with him each day in prayer and Bible reading, better preparing you for the battles of this life and equipping you to help others through their own difficult times.

I leave you with this prayer of blessing that Paul prayed over the Ephesians: "I keep asking that the God of our Lord Jesus Christ, the glorious Father, may give you the Spirit of wisdom and revelation, so that you may know him better. I pray also that the eyes of your heart may be enlightened in order that you may know the hope to which he has called you, the riches of his glorious inheritance in the saints, and his incomparably great power for us who believe" (Ephesians 1:17–19).

Appendix A

Prayer Journal Layout

This layout will get you started with your prayer journal. You will have many prayer requests over the years, so I recommend using a notebook to use as your journal. I set mine up by devoting a section to each day of the week, Sunday through Saturday. For each day of the week, I record my prayer requests with their dates on one page, and the answers to those prayers with their dates on the page opposite.

(left-side page)   (right-side page)

SUNDAY

Date	Prayer Request	Date	Answer

1.
2.
3.
4.
5.
6.
7.
8.
9.
10.

Appendix B

Thirty Days of Bible Reading: The Gospel of John

Day 1 John 1:1–28
Day 2 John 1:29–50
Day 3 John 2
Day 4 John 3:1–36
Day 5 John 4:1–26
Day 6 John 4:27–54
Day 7 John 5:1–30
Day 8 John 5:31–47
Day 9 John 6:1–21
Day 10 John 6:22–59
Day 11 John 6:60–7:24
Day 12 John 7:25–53
Day 13 John 8:1–30
Day 14 John 8:31–58
Day 15 John 9
Day 16 John 10
Day 17 John 11:1–37
Day 18 John 11:38–57
Day 19 John 12:1–19
Day 20 John 12:20–50
Day 21 John 13
Day 22 John 14
Day 23 John 15
Day 24 John 16
Day 25 John 17

Day 26 John 18
Day 27 John 19:1–27
Day 28 John 19:28–42
Day 29 John 20
Day 30 John 21

Appendix C

Three Months of Bible Reading: The New Testament

This plan is available online at http://www.hpfc.org. "Bible Reading Plan", then follow the link for "New Testament in 90 days".

Appendix D

Two-Year Chronological Bible Reading Plan

This plan is available on www.hpfc.org. Click on "Bible Reading Plan" and then follow the link for "Daily Bible Reading plan in Chronological for Old Testament (which is read over two years) & New Testament (which is read once a year) except Psalms and Proverbs which are included in the daily reading plan".

The plan was created by Doug Bartsch based on the "Chronological" one-year reading guide at www.backtothebible.org.